WINTER'S TALE
SHAKESPEARE FOR KIDS

JEANETTE VIGON

Copyright © 2023 Jeanette Vigon
All rights reserved.
ISBN: 9798332461934

CONTENTS

Why I wrote this book the way I did	vii
Introduction	ix
ACT I	1
Scene 1	3
Scene 2	7
ACT II	27
Scene 1	29
Scene 2	39
Scene 3	45
ACT III	55
Scene 1	57
Scene 2	59
Scene 3	69
ACT IV	75
Scene 1	77
Scene 2	79
Scene 3	83
Scene 4	91
ACT V	127
Scene 1	129
Scene 2	141
Scene 3	149
The Life of William Shakespeare	157
Afterword	161
Shakespeare for Kids - Other books in the series	163

This book is a modern adaptation for children of William Shakespeare's "Winter's Tale," a work in the public domain. While retaining the original story's essence and characters, this version has significant original content designed for young readers. It includes simplified language and reimagined scenes to make the profound tale accessible and engaging for children. The adaptation respects Shakespeare's original work's essence while presenting it in a relatable and understandable manner for a younger audience. The goal is to introduce children to this classic story in a friendly and engaging way.

Why I Wrote This Book The Way I Did

When I embarked on the journey of adapting Shakespeare's plays for children, my primary goal was to bridge the gap between the timeless allure of Shakespeare's narratives and the imaginative worlds of young readers. The decision to adapt these plays for children was driven by a desire to introduce them to the richness of literary classics at an early age, fostering a love for literature that could grow with them.

Choosing to maintain the original structure of acts and scenes was a deliberate effort to preserve the integrity and rhythm of Shakespeare's works. This approach not only honors the original compositions but also introduces young readers to the conventions of drama and the beauty of structured storytelling. It was important to me that children experience the plays as they were intended, albeit in a more accessible form.

Incorporating literary language while ensuring it remains engaging and understandable for children was a balancing act. I aimed to simplify the complexity of Shakespeare's language without diluting its power and beauty. By carefully selecting vocabulary and crafting sentences that convey the essence of the original plays, I aspired to captivate young minds and stimulate their intellectual curiosity.

Adapting these plays also involved making thoughtful choices about content, ensuring that themes and scenes were appropriate for a young audience. This required a sensitive approach to storytelling, where the lessons of love, loyalty, betrayal, and justice are presented in a manner that is both educational and entertaining.

In summary, the creation of this book was a labor of love, guided by the belief that Shakespeare's works are not just for adults but for everyone. By adapting these plays for children, I hope to plant the seeds of appreciation for classic literature in the fertile ground of young imaginations, encouraging a lifelong journey of reading, learning, and discovery.

I truly hope you will enjoy reading it, as much as I enjoyed re-writing it.

INTRODUCTION

Welcome to the wintery and magical world of "The Winter's Tale," where we journey to a realm of kings and queens, mysterious lands, and heartwarming reunions. This isn't just a story of royal jealousy and redemption; it's a tale of friendship, miracles, and the enduring power of love and forgiveness.

Our adventure begins in the kingdom of Sicilia, where King Leontes' unfounded jealousy sets off a chain of events that leads to sorrow and loss. But in this world, where the chill of winter gives way to the promise of spring, there is always hope for renewal and joy.

At the heart of this tale is the innocent and virtuous Queen Hermione, who faces great trials with grace and strength.

INTRODUCTION

Her story intertwines with that of her daughter, Perdita, lost but found again, who grows up unaware of her royal heritage in the shepherd's fields of Bohemia.

But fear not, for this epic is also brimming with enchantment and excitement. There are magical transformations, a living statue, and unexpected reunions that warm the heart. Amidst the drama, there are lessons of forgiveness, resilience, and the unbreakable bonds of family.

So, get ready to embark on a journey through "The Winter's Tale" in a way that's perfect for kids. Imagine grand palaces and humble shepherds' cottages, a world where statues come to life, and learning about the importance of faith, hope, and reconciliation.

Are you ready? Let's join Hermione, Perdita, and a host of fascinating characters, as we explore a story that has touched hearts for generations, now reimagined for young adventurers like you! Come along, into the magical world of "The Winter's Tale," where every twist of fate brings us closer to understanding the true meaning of love and forgiveness!

ACT I

SCENE 1

Camillo and Archidamus walked through the antechamber of Leontes' palace, engaged in conversation.

"If you ever visit Bohemia, Camillo," Archidamus said, "you will see a big difference between our Bohemia and your Sicilia."

Camillo nodded. "This summer, I think the King of Sicilia plans to visit Bohemia. He owes your king a visit."

. . .

Archidamus smiled. "We will welcome him with all the love we have, though our hospitality might not match yours. We might even give you sleepy drinks so you won't notice our shortcomings."

Camillo chuckled. "You are too kind. You give so much for what should be free."

Archidamus shook his head. "I speak honestly. We might not be as grand as you, but we do our best."

"Sicilia and Bohemia have a strong bond," Camillo said. "The kings grew up together, and their affection for each other has only grown. Even though they are apart, they exchange gifts and letters. It's as if they are still together, shaking hands and embracing across the distance. May their friendship last forever!"

"I believe nothing can change their friendship," Archidamus agreed. "You must be very proud of your young prince Mamillius. He is a promising young gentleman."

. . .

Camillo beamed. "Yes, he is a wonderful child. He brings joy to everyone. Even the old people feel young again when they see him. They want to live longer just to watch him grow up."

"Would they be content to die otherwise?" Archidamus asked.

"Yes," Camillo replied. "If they had no other reason to live, they would still want to see the prince grow."

"If the king had no son, they would wish to live on crutches until he had one," Archidamus said with a laugh.

With that, the two men exited the antechamber, their conversation drifting into the corridors of the palace.

SCENE 2

In a grand room of the palace, Leontes, the king, was with his queen Hermione, their young son Mamillius, and their friend Polixenes, the king of Bohemia. Camillo and attendants were also present.

Polixenes said, "Nine months have passed since I left my throne. I should thank you for your hospitality, my brother, but I feel I can never fully repay you. So, with one 'thank you,' I multiply my gratitude a thousand times."

Leontes replied, "Hold your thanks for now and give them when you leave."

. . .

Polixenes answered, "But that's tomorrow. I'm worried about what might happen in my absence. Besides, I've stayed long enough to tire you out."

Leontes reassured him, "We are tougher than you think, brother."

Polixenes insisted, "No, I must leave tomorrow."

Leontes pleaded, "Stay one more week."

Polixenes shook his head. "I truly must go tomorrow."

Leontes then offered, "Let's split the difference and make it three more days."

Polixenes, with a heavy heart, said, "Please don't press me. No one else's words would persuade me as much as yours, but my affairs pull me home. Staying longer would be a burden to both of us. Farewell, brother."

. . .

Leontes noticed Hermione's silence and said, "Why so quiet, my queen? Speak."

Hermione said, "I thought I'd wait until you had convinced him not to leave. You aren't trying hard enough. Tell him everything is fine in Bohemia; that would satisfy him."

Leontes responded, "Well said, Hermione."

Hermione continued, "Tell him he misses his son. If he admits that, let him go. But make him swear he's telling the truth, and we'll let him leave."

She then addressed Polixenes, "I ask for just one more week. When you return to Bohemia, I'll allow my lord to stay there for a month. You'll stay, won't you?"

Polixenes replied, "No, madam."

Hermione pressed, "But you will, won't you?"

. . .

Polixenes firmly said, "I really can't."

Hermione teased, "You try to put me off with excuses, but I'll still say, 'You shall not go.' A lady's 'You shall not go' is as strong as a lord's. Will you stay now? Do I have to keep you here as a prisoner instead of a guest?"

Polixenes relented, "I'll be your guest, madam. Being your prisoner would mean I've done something wrong."

Hermione smiled, "Not your jailer, then, but your kind hostess. Come, I'll ask you about my lord's tricks when you were boys. You were playful little lords, weren't you?"

Polixenes reminisced, "We were two boys who thought each day was just like the next, and we would stay boys forever."

Hermione asked, "Wasn't my lord the more mischievous one?"

. . .

Polixenes laughed, "We were like twin lambs playing in the sun, innocent and unaware of any wrongdoing. If we had stayed that way, we could have faced heaven boldly and said we were not guilty."

Hermione added, "So you've made mistakes since then?"

Polixenes sighed, "Temptations have come since those days. Back then, my wife was just a girl, and your lovely face hadn't yet graced my friend's eyes."

Hermione replied, "Grace be with us! Don't conclude that your queen and I are bad influences. If we've led you astray, we'll take the blame, but only if you never sinned with anyone else."

Leontes asked, "Is he persuaded yet?"

Hermione smiled, "He'll stay, my lord."

. . .

Leontes, feeling frustrated, said, "He wouldn't stay for me, but he will for you. My dear, you've never spoken so well."

Hermione teased, "Never?"

Leontes replied, "Only once before."

Hermione asked, "When was that? Please, tell me. Praise me and make me happy. Our praises are our rewards."

Leontes recalled, "That was when it took three hard months to win you over and make you agree to be my wife. Then you said, 'I am yours forever.'"

Hermione smiled, "That was indeed a special moment. So, I've spoken well twice: once to gain a husband and once to keep a friend."

Leontes, thinking privately, "This is too much! Their friendship looks too intimate. It makes me uneasy. Mamillius, are you my boy?"

. . .

Mamillius answered, "Yes, my good lord."

Leontes watched Mamillius, smiling. "I fecks!" he exclaimed. "Why, that's my boy. Have you smudged your nose? They say it looks just like mine. Come, captain, we must be neat and clean."

Mamillius looked up at him, "Yes, my lord."

Leontes chuckled, "You need a rougher look to be fully like me. Yet they say we are almost as alike as eggs. Women say that, and they might be lying, but still, it's true enough to say this boy looks like me. Come, young man, look at me. Sweet rascal! Can it be possible?" He was lost in thought, trying to understand his emotions. "Feelings make us believe impossible things. How can this be real?" He was deep in his suspicions, thinking the worst of his wife.

Polixenes noticed something was wrong. "What's the matter, Sicilia?" he asked.

. . .

Hermione also noticed and said, "He seems troubled."

Polixenes asked again, "What's wrong, my lord? How are you, brother?"

Hermione looked worried. "You look very distracted. Are you okay, my lord?"

Leontes quickly said, "No, I'm fine. Sometimes our nature shows its foolish side. Looking at my boy's face, I felt like I went back twenty-three years and saw myself as a child. I was in my green velvet coat, with my dagger safely kept so it wouldn't harm me. I thought I looked so much like this little one. My honest friend, would you take eggs for money?"

Mamillius, trying to be brave, said, "No, my lord, I'll fight."

Leontes laughed, "You will! Why, that's good! My brother, do you love your young prince as much as we love ours?"

. . .

Polixenes nodded, "If I were at home, sir, he's everything to me—my joy, my friend, sometimes my enemy, my follower, my soldier, statesman, everything. He makes long days short, and his playful nature cures my worries."

Leontes said, "That's how this little one is for me. We'll go for a walk, my lord, and leave you to your important matters. Hermione, show our brother how much we love him by making him feel welcome. He is as dear to me as you and our young son."

Hermione smiled, "If you need us, we'll be in the garden. Shall we join you there?"

Leontes replied, "Go where you like; you'll be found under the sky." He spoke aside to himself, "I'm testing her now, though she doesn't see it." Watching Hermione with Polixenes, he fumed, "Look how she raises her face to him and acts bold, like a wife should to her husband!"

As Polixenes, Hermione, and the attendants left, Leontes fumed, "Gone already! This is too much! Go, play, boy, play. Your mother plays too, but in a disgraceful way that will bring me shame. Go, play, boy, play. There have been unfaithful wives before. Many men hold their wives' hands, not knowing they've been unfaithful. There's some comfort in knowing other men suffer the same. If every man with a cheating wife despaired, many would hang themselves. There's no cure for it; it's a common problem. How now, boy?"

Mamillius said, "They say I'm like you."

Leontes found a small comfort in that. "That's some comfort. What, Camillo, are you there?"

Camillo answered, "Yes, my good lord."

Leontes said, "Go play, Mamillius; you're a good boy."

After Mamillius left, Leontes turned to Camillo. "This great man will stay longer."

. . .

Camillo noted, "You had a hard time making him stay. When you tried, he kept wanting to leave."

Leontes asked, "Did you notice it?"

Camillo replied, "He wouldn't stay for your requests. He made his business seem more important."

Leontes continued, "Did you see it? People are already whispering about it. How did it happen, Camillo, that he stayed?"

Camillo explained, "At the queen's request."

Leontes, feeling betrayed, said, "At the queen's request, indeed. It was noticed by no one but you?"

Camillo confirmed, "Most understand that Bohemia stays longer."

. . .

Leontes, feeling his jealousy grow, asked, "Why?"

Camillo responded, "To please your highness and the queen."

Leontes, in disbelief, said, "The queen's requests! I trusted you, Camillo, with my deepest secrets. But now I see I was wrong."

Camillo, shocked, said, "God forbid, my lord!"

Leontes accused him, "You are either dishonest or a coward, not acting as you should. Or maybe you're a fool who sees the truth but takes it lightly."

Camillo tried to defend himself, "My gracious lord, everyone makes mistakes. If I have been negligent, it was foolishness, not weighing the end result. If I have been fearful, it was the fear that often affects the wisest. But please, tell me my fault plainly."

. . .

Leontes asked, "Haven't you seen that my wife is unfaithful? If you deny it, you're blind. Say my wife is unfaithful and justify it."

Camillo was horrified. "I wouldn't stand by and hear the queen insulted without taking action. You have never spoken less appropriately."

Leontes angrily retorted, "Is whispering nothing? Is meeting faces and kissing nothing? Is sneaking around nothing? If this is nothing, then everything is nothing. My wife is nothing, and so is everything else if this is nothing."

Camillo pleaded, "My lord, please get rid of this dangerous thought."

Leontes stubbornly said, "Say it's dangerous, but it's true."

Camillo denied, "No, my lord."

. . .

Leontes, feeling betrayed, said, "It is. You lie, Camillo. I hate you. Either you see both good and evil and choose both, or you're dishonest."

Camillo asked, "Who has infected her?"

Leontes replied, "He who wears her like a medal, Bohemia. If I had true servants, they would see my honor and take action. Even you, his cupbearer, might put something in his drink to give him a lasting sleep. That drink would be a relief to me."

Camillo, stunned, said, "I could do it with a potion, but I can't believe my honorable queen is unfaithful."

Leontes dismissed him, "Go rot! Do you think I would bring this upon myself without reason?"

Camillo, now convinced of Leontes' belief, said, "I must believe you, sir. I will take care of Bohemia, but when he's gone, you must take back your queen for your son's sake."

. . .

Leontes agreed, "You advise as I've planned. I won't tarnish her honor."

Camillo said, "Go and keep a friendly face with Bohemia and the queen. I'll make sure Bohemia has a safe drink. If not, don't count me as your servant."

Leontes replied, "Do it, and you have my heart. Don't, and you'll regret it."

Camillo agreed, "I'll do it, my lord."

Leontes left, saying, "I will seem friendly, as you advised."

Camillo, left alone, lamented, "Poor lady! But what should I do? I must poison Polixenes, obeying a master who is at war with himself. If there were examples of people who killed kings and thrived, I might do it. But there are none. I must leave the court. Doing this would be my downfall. Happy star, guide me!"

· · ·

Polixenes re-entered, puzzled. "This is strange. I feel my favor here is fading. Good day, Camillo."

Camillo greeted him, "Hail, most royal sir!"

Polixenes asked, "What's the news at court?"

Camillo replied, "None rare, my lord."

Polixenes noted, "The king looks like he's lost something precious. He left me in contempt. What's causing this change?"

Camillo hesitated, "I dare not know, my lord."

Polixenes pressed, "How! Dare not! You must know and dare not tell me?"

Camillo sighed, "I cannot name the disease, but it is caught from you who are well."

. . .

Polixenes, confused, asked, "Caught from me? Make me not like the basilisk, killing with a look. If you know something, tell me."

Camillo, feeling the pressure, said, "I may not answer."

Polixenes insisted, "I must be answered. What harm is coming toward me? How far off, how near? How can it be prevented?"

Camillo decided to tell him, "I am supposed to murder you."

Polixenes, shocked, asked, "By whom?"

Camillo replied, "By the king."

Polixenes asked, "Why?"

. . .

Camillo explained, "He thinks you have touched his queen inappropriately."

Polixenes, horrified, said, "If that's true, let my best blood turn to jelly. Let my name be ruined. Let my approach be shunned."

Camillo assured him, "No oath or counsel can change the king's mind. His belief is unshakeable."

Polixenes asked, "How did this happen?"

Camillo replied, "I don't know, but it's safer to avoid danger than question its origin. If you trust my honesty, leave tonight. I'll help you and your followers escape. For myself, I'll leave the court. Do not hesitate; my parents' honor is at stake. If you try to prove this, I won't stand by you. You will be condemned by the king."

. . .

Polixenes believed him, "I saw his anger. Give me your hand. Be my guide. My ships are ready. This jealousy is for a precious woman and must be strong. Let's go, Camillo."

Camillo said, "I can command the keys. Take the urgent hour. Come, sir, away."

They both exited, preparing to flee.

ACT II

SCENE 1

In a room in Leontes' palace, Hermione was with Mamillius and some ladies. She handed Mamillius over to one of the ladies. "Take the boy, he troubles me so much, it's more than I can bear."

One of the ladies, trying to cheer him up, asked, "Come, my gracious lord, shall I be your playmate?"

Mamillius firmly said, "No, I don't want you."

The lady, puzzled, asked, "Why not, my sweet lord?"

. . .

Mamillius replied, "You'll kiss me too hard and talk to me like I'm still a baby. I like you better."

Another lady, curious, asked, "And why is that, my lord?"

Mamillius explained, "Not because your eyebrows are darker. Though they say dark eyebrows suit some women best, as long as there's not too much hair and they make a nice shape."

The lady, surprised, asked, "Who taught you this?"

Mamillius answered, "I learned it from looking at women's faces. What color are your eyebrows?"

The first lady teased, "Blue, my lord."

Mamillius laughed, "No, that's a joke. I've seen a lady with a blue nose, but not blue eyebrows."

. . .

The first lady smiled, "Listen, your mother, the queen, is expecting a new baby. Soon, you'll have a new playmate if we would let you."

The second lady added, "She's getting quite large lately. It's nearly time."

Hermione interrupted their conversation, "What are you talking about? Come here, sir, I'm ready for you again. Please, sit with us and tell us a story."

Mamillius asked, "Should it be a happy or sad tale?"

Hermione replied, "As happy as you like."

Mamillius decided, "A sad tale is best for winter. I have one about ghosts and goblins."

Hermione encouraged him, "Let's hear it, good sir. Come, sit down. Do your best to scare me with your ghosts. You're good at it."

. . .

Mamillius began, "There was a man—"

Hermione interrupted, "No, come, sit down first, then start."

Mamillius continued, "He lived by a graveyard. I'll tell it quietly so the crickets won't hear."

Hermione urged him, "Come on, then, whisper it in my ear."

Leontes entered with Antigonus, lords, and other attendants. He was in a rage. "Did you see him? Was Camillo with him?"

A lord answered, "I saw them behind the pines. They were hurrying to their ships."

Leontes, feeling vindicated, said, "I'm glad my suspicions were right. Knowing less would be a curse. Sometimes, not knowing about the danger is better. But once you see the danger, it's too late. I've seen the danger and Camillo helped him escape. There's a plot against my life and crown. Everything I feared is true. How were the gates opened so easily?"

The lord explained, "With Camillo's authority. Your command often allows that."

Leontes acknowledged, "I know it too well. Give me the boy. I'm glad you didn't nurse him. Though he resembles me, he has too much of your blood."

Hermione, confused, asked, "Is this a joke?"

Leontes angrily ordered, "Take the boy away. He won't come near her. She can amuse herself with the child she carries. It's Polixenes who made her pregnant."

Hermione, hurt and defensive, replied, "I would say he didn't, and I swear you would believe me, no matter your doubts."

. . .

Leontes addressed the lords, "Look at her closely. You might say she's a good woman, but your honesty would add it's a pity she's not virtuous. Praise her outward beauty, which deserves high praise, and soon you'd hesitate to say she's honorable. I, who have the most reason to grieve, say she's an adulteress."

Hermione, holding back tears, said, "If a villain said that, he'd be the greatest villain. You, my lord, are mistaken."

Leontes retorted, "You mistook Polixenes for Leontes. You adulteress! A traitor with Camillo, who helped you escape. You are as bad as those who get the worst titles."

Hermione protested, "No, by my life, I knew nothing of this. When you realize the truth, you'll regret saying this about me. Gentle lord, you can only right this wrong by admitting your mistake."

Leontes, unmoved, ordered, "No! If my foundation is wrong, then nothing can stand. Take her away! To prison! Anyone who defends her is guilty too."

. . .

Hermione, resigned, said, "There's some bad fate ruling now. I must be patient until better times. My lords, I don't cry easily, as most women do, so you may not pity me. But I feel a grief that burns worse than tears. Measure me with your charity, and fulfill the king's will."

Leontes snapped, "Shall I be heard?"

Hermione asked, "Who will go with me? My ladies need to come; you see my condition requires it. Don't cry, my friends. There's no reason to. If you find out I deserve prison, then cry. This action is for my better grace. Farewell, my lord. I never wished to see you sorrowful, but now I trust I shall. My ladies, come; you have permission."

Leontes ordered, "Go, do our bidding; hence!"

After Hermione exited, guarded by her ladies, the first lord pleaded, "Please, your highness, call the queen back."

Antigonus warned, "Be certain of what you do, sir. Your

justice could turn into violence, harming yourself, your queen, and your son."

The first lord added, "I'd stake my life that the queen is innocent in the eyes of heaven and you."

Antigonus said, "If she's guilty, I'd keep my wife in the stables and never trust her. Every inch of woman in the world would be false."

Leontes, dismissing them, said, "Hold your tongues."

The first lord insisted, "Good my lord—"

Antigonus continued, "We speak for you, not ourselves. You are deceived by someone who will be damned for it. If I knew the villain, I'd destroy him. If the queen is dishonorable, I have three daughters. If this is true, they'll pay for it. I'd rather be castrated than let them produce false offspring."

. . .

Leontes ordered, "Cease, no more. You sense this matter as coldly as a dead man. I see and feel it clearly."

Antigonus replied, "If that's true, honesty has no place left in the world."

Leontes asked, "Do you doubt me?"

The first lord said, "I'd rather you doubted than I. I want her honor to be true more than I care about your suspicion."

Leontes, frustrated, said, "Why do we need to discuss this? Our prerogative doesn't require your counsel. If you can't accept the truth, inform yourselves; we need no more advice. This matter is ours alone."

Antigonus wished, "I wish you had judged this quietly without more action."

Leontes retorted, "How could that be? You must be ignorant or foolish. Camillo's flight, added to their familiarity, proves my case. I've sent to Apollo's temple for confirmation. Cleomenes and Dion will bring back the truth. Have I done well?"

The first lord agreed, "Well done, my lord."

Leontes, though convinced, added, "I am satisfied, but the oracle will confirm it for others. We've confined her to prevent her from fulfilling the traitors' plans. Come, follow us; we must speak publicly."

Antigonus, aside, thought, "To laughter, if the truth were known."

They all exited, with Leontes determined to prove his accusations.

SCENE 2

In a dark prison, Paulina arrived with a gentleman and some attendants. She called out, "Fetch the keeper of the prison. Let him know who I am."

The gentleman left to find the keeper, while Paulina muttered, "Good lady, no court in Europe is too good for you. What are you doing in prison?"

The gentleman returned with the gaoler, who greeted Paulina respectfully. "Do you know me?" Paulina asked.

. . .

The gaoler replied, "Of course, you are a worthy lady, one I honor greatly."

Paulina said, "Then please, take me to the queen."

The gaoler hesitated. "I can't, madam. I have strict orders against it."

Paulina, frustrated, said, "Is there any way I can see her women? What about Emilia?"

The gaoler nodded, "If you ask your attendants to wait aside, I will bring Emilia to you."

Paulina agreed, "Call her then. Everyone else, step aside."

The gentleman and attendants left, and the gaoler went to fetch Emilia, but insisted, "I must be present during your meeting."

. . .

Paulina relented, "Fine, be it so."

After a short wait, the gaoler returned with Emilia. Paulina greeted her warmly, "Dear gentlewoman, how is our gracious lady?"

Emilia sighed, "As well as one so great and so forsaken can be. She has endured much fear and grief. She gave birth early."

Paulina asked, "A boy?"

Emilia replied, "A daughter, a healthy baby. The queen finds great comfort in her, saying, 'My poor prisoner, I am as innocent as you.'"

Paulina, indignant, said, "The king's madness must be addressed. He needs to be told, and I will do it. If I speak gently, let my tongue blister. Emilia, tell the queen that if she trusts me with her baby, I'll show it to the king and plead her case. He might soften at the sight of the child. Innocence often persuades when words fail."

. . .

Emilia, grateful, said, "You are the best person for this task. The queen thought of this plan today but dared not ask anyone for fear of rejection. I will tell her at once."

Paulina reassured her, "Tell her I will do my best. If my words are as bold as my heart, I will succeed."

Emilia blessed Paulina, "May you be blessed for this! Come closer, I will inform the queen."

The gaoler, worried, said, "Madam, if the queen sends the baby, I might get in trouble for allowing it without a warrant."

Paulina confidently replied, "You need not fear. This child was a prisoner in the womb but is now free by nature's law. She is not part of the king's anger nor guilty of any crime. Trust me, I will protect you from any danger."

. . .

The gaoler nodded, believing her. "I do believe it."

Paulina assured him, "Do not worry. I will stand between you and any harm."

With that, they all exited to carry out their plans.

SCENE 3

In a room in Leontes' palace, the king was pacing, unable to find peace. "Neither night nor day do I rest. It is weak of me to bear this matter so. If the cause did not exist—if she, the adulteress, did not exist, some peace might come back to me. Who's there?"

A servant stepped forward, "My lord?"

Leontes asked, "How is the boy?"

The servant replied, "He slept well last night; we hope his sickness is gone."

. . .

Leontes, pained, said, "To see his nobleness! Understanding his mother's dishonor, he quickly declined, drooped, and took it deeply. He fasted, lost his spirit, appetite, and sleep, and grew weak. Leave me; go see how he is."

The servant exited, and Leontes muttered to himself, "Fie, fie! No thought of him now. My revenge will have to wait; he's too powerful and well-connected. But for now, I can take it out on her. Camillo and Polixenes laugh at me, but she is within my reach."

Paulina entered, carrying a baby. The first lord tried to stop her, "You must not enter."

Paulina insisted, "No, my lords, help me. Do you fear his wrath more than the queen's life? She is innocent and more virtuous than he is jealous."

Antigonus added, "That's enough."

. . .

A second servant explained, "Madam, he hasn't slept and commanded that no one should come near him."

Paulina, undeterred, said, "I bring him sleep. You, who sigh at every unnecessary breath he takes, only feed his wakefulness. I come with honest words to purge him of his distress."

Leontes heard the commotion. "What noise is this?"

Paulina answered, "No noise, my lord, just necessary talk about some matters for your highness."

Leontes, furious, commanded, "Away with that audacious lady! Antigonus, I told you she should not come near me."

Antigonus apologized, "I told her so, my lord, on pain of your displeasure and mine."

Leontes barked, "What, can't you control her?"

. . .

Paulina boldly replied, "In everything but this. Unless he acts as you do, condemning honor, he cannot rule me."

Antigonus sighed, "You hear her, my lord. She takes the reins when she wants, but she doesn't stumble."

Paulina addressed Leontes, "My liege, I come as your loyal servant, your healer, your obedient counselor. I come from your good queen."

Leontes scoffed, "Good queen!"

Paulina insisted, "Good queen, my lord. I say good queen. Were I a man, I'd defend her honor with combat."

Leontes, enraged, ordered, "Force her out."

Paulina challenged, "Let anyone who belittles his eyes hand me first. I'll leave willingly, but I must do my errand. The good queen, for she is good, has given you a daughter. Here she is, and she sends her for your blessing."

Paulina laid the baby down. Leontes, furious, shouted, "Out! You witch! Out of my sight, you meddling woman!"

Paulina defended herself, "I am as ignorant of any wrongdoing as you are in falsely accusing me. I am as honest as you are mad, which is enough in this world to pass for honesty."

Leontes called his lords, "Traitors! Will you not push her out? Give her the bastard. You are controlled by your wives. Take the bastard and give it to your old woman."

Paulina fiercely responded, "May your hands never be revered if you take up the princess with such baseless accusations!"

Leontes sneered, "He fears his wife."

Paulina retorted, "I wish you did. Then you would call your children your own."

. . .

Leontes, feeling betrayed, declared, "A nest of traitors!"

Antigonus protested, "I am no traitor, by this light."

Paulina added, "Nor I, nor anyone but you. You betray your honor, your queen's, your son's, and your baby's to slander. Slander is sharper than a sword and you refuse to remove your rotten opinion."

Leontes, furious, called her names, "A woman with a boundless tongue! This brat is none of mine; it is Polixenes'. Burn it and its mother!"

Paulina declared, "It is yours. My lords, look at the baby. She has her father's eyes, nose, lips, even his frown, and dimples. Nature has made her so like you that if she had control of the mind, there would be no suspicion."

Leontes, seething, shouted, "You deserve to be hanged for not silencing her."

. . .

Antigonus replied, "If all husbands who couldn't control their wives were hanged, you'd have few subjects left."

Leontes, in a fit of rage, demanded, "Take her away!"

Paulina stood her ground, "An unworthy and unnatural lord can do no more harm."

Leontes threatened, "I'll have you burnt."

Paulina, undaunted, said, "It is a heretic that makes the fire, not she who burns in it. I won't call you a tyrant, but this cruel treatment of your queen shows your weak mind and will make you infamous."

Leontes ordered, "Out of the chamber with her! Were I a tyrant, she wouldn't dare call me one. Away with her!"

. . .

Paulina, leaving, said, "Don't push me; I'll go. Look after your baby, my lord. She is yours. May Jove send her a better guiding spirit! You, who are so tender over his follies, will never do him any good. Farewell."

As she exited, Leontes fumed, "You, traitor, have set your wife on this. Take the child and burn it. Do it immediately, or I'll take your life and everything you have. If you refuse, I'll smash its brains out myself. Take it to the fire; you set your wife on this."

Antigonus, pleading, said, "I did not, sir. These lords can clear me."

The lords supported him, "We can, my royal liege. He is not guilty of her coming here."

Leontes, still distrustful, accused them, "You're all liars."

The first lord begged, "Please, your highness, trust us. We have always served you faithfully. We beg you to change this terrible plan, which will lead to a horrible outcome."

. . .

Leontes, feeling the pressure, said, "I am swayed by every wind. Shall I live to see this bastard call me father? Better to burn it now than curse it later. But let it live. It shall not. You, come here. You who have been so tender with Lady Margery, your midwife, to save this bastard's life—what will you do to save it?"

Antigonus offered, "Anything, my lord, within my power. At least, I'll risk my own life to save the innocent."

Leontes commanded, "Swear by this sword that you will do my bidding."

Antigonus swore, "I will, my lord."

Leontes warned, "Fail in any point, and it will mean death for you and your wife. Take this female bastard to a remote place outside our dominions. Leave it to the mercy of the elements. As it came to us by strange fortune, I charge you to abandon it. Take it up."

. . .

Antigonus, heartbroken, said, "I swear to do this, though a quick death would be more merciful. Come on, poor babe. May some spirit guide you. Wolves and bears have shown pity. Sir, may you prosper more than this deed requires. Blessing against this cruelty fight on your side, poor thing."

He exited with the child. Leontes muttered, "No, I'll not raise another's child."

A servant entered. "Your highness, the messengers from the oracle have returned. Cleomenes and Dion have landed and are hastening to the court."

The first lord added, "Their speed has been remarkable."

Leontes, hopeful, said, "They've been gone twenty-three days. Apollo will reveal the truth. Prepare, lords. We will give our queen a fair and open trial. As long as she lives, my heart will be burdened. Leave me and think upon my bidding."

The lords exited, leaving Leontes to brood over his decisions.

ACT III

SCENE 1

Cleomenes and Dion arrived at the seaport in Sicilia, full of wonder from their journey.

Cleomenes marveled, "The climate is so delicate, the air is sweet, the island fertile, and the temple far surpasses its already high praise."

Dion nodded in agreement, adding, "What impressed me the most were the celestial robes and the reverence of the priests. Oh, and the sacrifice! It was so ceremonious, solemn, and otherworldly."

. . .

Cleomenes agreed, "But above all, the powerful and deafening voice of the oracle, like Jove's thunder, overwhelmed my senses completely."

Dion hoped, "If the outcome of our journey proves as successful for the queen—oh, let it be so!—as it was pleasant and speedy for us, then the time spent is well worth it."

Cleomenes prayed, "Great Apollo, turn all to the best! I dislike these accusations against Hermione."

Dion observed, "The forceful way this has been handled will either clear her or end the matter. When the oracle's message, sealed by Apollo, is revealed, something extraordinary will come to light. Let's get fresh horses and hope for a favorable outcome!"

With that, they prepared to leave, hopeful for a positive resolution.

SCENE 2

In a grand court of justice, Leontes, lords, and officers gathered. The air was thick with tension as Leontes spoke.

"This session, to our great grief, we pronounce, even pushes against our heart: the party tried is the daughter of a king, our wife, and one we loved too much. Let us be cleared of being tyrannous, as we proceed in justice, which shall have due course, even to the guilt or the purgation. Produce the prisoner."

An officer announced, "It is his highness' pleasure that the queen appear in person here in court. Silence!"

Hermione entered, guarded, with Paulina and other ladies attending her. Leontes ordered, "Read the indictment."

The officer read aloud, "Hermione, queen to the worthy Leontes, king of Sicilia, you are accused and arraigned of high treason, committing adultery with Polixenes, king of Bohemia, and conspiring with Camillo to take the life of our sovereign lord the king. You did counsel and aid them to flee by night."

Hermione, standing tall, responded, "Since what I say must contradict my accusation, and the testimony on my part is only mine, it may scarcely help to say 'not guilty.' My integrity, being called falsehood, will be received as such. But if divine powers behold our actions, as they do, I doubt not but innocence shall make false accusation blush and tyranny tremble. My past life has been as chaste, as true, as I am now unhappy. A fellow of the royal bed, a great king's daughter, the mother to a hopeful prince, I stand here to talk for life and honor. For life, I prize it as I weigh grief, which I would spare: for honor, it is from me to mine, and only that I stand for. I appeal to your conscience, sir. Before Polixenes came to your court, how was I in your grace? Since he came, what has happened to make me appear thus? If I have gone beyond the bounds of honor, harden all hearts against me, and let my closest kin cry 'shame' upon my grave."

Leontes, unmoved, retorted, "I never heard yet that these bold vices lacked the impudence to deny what they did."

Hermione replied, "That may be true, but it does not apply to me."

Leontes accused, "You will not own your actions."

Hermione defended herself, "I must not acknowledge any fault. For Polixenes, with whom I am accused, I confess I loved him as honor required, with the same kind of love as you commanded. Not to have done so would have been disobedience and ingratitude to you and to your friend. As for conspiracy, I know nothing of it. Camillo was an honest man; why he left your court, the gods themselves know no more than I do."

· · ·

Leontes accused her further, "You knew of his departure and what you undertook in his absence."

Hermione responded, "You speak a language I do not understand. My life stands in the shadow of your dreams, which I will lay down."

Leontes, consumed by his suspicions, declared, "Your actions are my dreams; you had a bastard by Polixenes, and I dreamt it. You were past all shame and truth. Your child has been cast out; so shall you be, and you will face justice, with the least punishment being death."

Hermione, unafraid, said, "Spare your threats. Life is no longer a commodity for me. The crown and comfort of my life, your favor, is gone. My second joy, my son, is barred from me. My third comfort, my newborn, has been taken and proclaimed a strumpet. I am denied the privileges of a new mother and hurried here before gaining strength. Tell me, my liege, what blessings do I have to live for? Proceed. But hear this: my life I do not prize, but my honor, which I would clear. If I am condemned on mere surmises and your jealousies, it is rigor and not law. I appeal to the oracle: Apollo be my judge!"

. . .

The first lord supported her request, "This is just. Bring forth Apollo's oracle."

Some officers exited to fetch the oracle, while Hermione lamented, "The Emperor of Russia was my father. If only he were alive to see my trial and my misery with eyes of pity."

The officers returned with Cleomenes and Dion. The officer instructed, "You shall swear upon this sword of justice that you, Cleomenes and Dion, have been to Delphos, and from there brought the sealed oracle, delivered by Apollo's priest, and that you have not dared to break the seal or read the contents."

Cleomenes and Dion swore, "We swear."

Leontes commanded, "Break the seals and read."

The officer read, "Hermione is chaste; Polixenes blameless; Camillo a true subject; Leontes a jealous tyrant; his innocent babe truly begotten; and the king shall live without an heir if that which is lost is not found."

The lords rejoiced, "Now blessed be the great Apollo!"

Hermione praised, "Praised!"

Leontes, in disbelief, asked, "Have you read the truth?"

The officer confirmed, "Yes, my lord, exactly as it is set down."

Leontes, refusing to believe, declared, "There is no truth in the oracle. The sessions shall proceed. This is mere falsehood."

A servant rushed in, "My lord, the king!"

Leontes asked, "What is the matter?"

. . .

The servant, hesitant, said, "O sir, I shall be hated to report it! The prince, your son, out of fear for the queen's fate, is dead."

Leontes, struck by the news, cried out, "How! gone!"

The servant confirmed, "He is dead."

Leontes, realizing his injustice, lamented, "Apollo is angry, and the heavens strike at my injustice."

Hermione swooned, and Paulina exclaimed, "This news is mortal to the queen: look down and see what death is doing."

Leontes, panicked, ordered, "Take her hence. Her heart is overcharged; she will recover. I have believed my own suspicions too much. Apply some remedies for life."

Paulina and the ladies carried Hermione out, and Leontes prayed, "Apollo, pardon my great profaneness against your oracle! I'll reconcile with Polixenes, woo my queen again, and recall the good Camillo. I proclaim him a man of truth and mercy. He revealed my plan to poison Polixenes and fled. How his honor shines through my jealousy!"

Paulina re-entered, heartbroken. "Woe the while! Cut my lace, lest my heart break."

The first lord asked, "What fit is this, good lady?"

Paulina, in despair, cried, "What torments, tyrant, do you have for me? Wheels? Racks? Fires? What torture must I endure, whose every word deserves the worst? Your tyranny, combined with your jealousy, has done more than any childish fancies. You betrayed Polixenes, wanted to poison Camillo, and cast your baby daughter to die. The death of your son is not laid at your feet, but the last—O lords, the queen, the sweetest creature, is dead."

The first lord prayed, "The higher powers forbid!"

. . .

Paulina insisted, "I say she is dead. Go and see. If there is any life in her, I'll serve you as I would the gods. But, tyrant, do not repent these things, for they are heavier than your woes. Despair is your only path. A thousand years of penance could not move the gods to look your way."

Leontes, overwhelmed with guilt, said, "Go on, go on. You cannot speak too much; I deserve all the bitterness."

The first lord cautioned, "Say no more. Whatever the outcome, you have been bold in your speech."

Paulina, calmer, said, "I am sorry for it. When I recognize my faults, I will repent. Alas! I have shown too much rashness. What is done is past help and should be past grief. Do not take affliction at my words. Now, good liege, forgive a foolish woman. The love I bore your queen—I'll speak of her no more, nor of your children. Take your patience and I'll say nothing."

Leontes, deeply remorseful, said, "You spoke well when you told the truth. Bring me to the bodies of my queen and son.

One grave shall hold them both. I will visit their resting place daily, and my tears will be my penance. Lead me to these sorrows."

They exited, leaving the court empty and heavy with the weight of their actions.

SCENE 3

In a remote, desolate area near the sea in Bohemia, Antigonus arrived with a child and a mariner.

Antigonus asked, "Are you sure our ship has landed in the deserts of Bohemia?"

The mariner replied, "Yes, my lord. But we have landed at a bad time. The skies look threatening, and a storm seems imminent. It feels like the heavens are angry with us for what we are about to do."

. . .

Antigonus sighed, "Their sacred wills be done! Go back to the ship and take care of it. I won't be long."

The mariner warned, "Make haste and don't go too far inland. The weather is likely to turn severe, and this place is known for wild creatures."

Antigonus assured him, "Go on; I'll follow soon."

The mariner, relieved to leave, said, "I'm glad to be rid of this business."

Left alone with the baby, Antigonus spoke softly, "Come, poor babe. I have heard of spirits returning, but I never believed it. Yet last night, I saw your mother. It wasn't a dream; it was too real. She appeared in pure white robes, looking sorrowful, and spoke to me. 'Good Antigonus,' she said, 'since fate has made you the one to abandon my poor child, take her to a remote place in Bohemia. Name her Perdita, for she is lost forever. And because of this cruel task given by my lord, you will never see your wife Paulina again.' With those words, she vanished. I was terrified but collected myself. Dreams are often foolish, yet this time I will heed it. I believe Hermione is dead, and Apollo has willed that this child, being Polixenes' issue, should be left here. Blossom, fare thee well!"

He laid the baby on the ground with some tokens. "Here, lie down. These things may help you if fortune is kind. The storm begins; poor wretch, you are exposed because of your mother's fault. I cannot weep, but my heart bleeds. Cursed am I to do this by oath. Farewell! The day grows darker. You will have a rough lullaby. I must get back to the ship. I am gone forever."

Antigonus exited, pursued by a bear.

A shepherd entered, muttering, "I wish there were no age between sixteen and twenty-three, or that youth would sleep through it, for it brings nothing but trouble: getting girls pregnant, wronging the elders, stealing, fighting. Hark, who hunts in this weather? They've scared away my best sheep. If they're anywhere, it's by the seaside. Good luck, what's this? Mercy, a baby! A very pretty baby! Is it a boy or girl? What an escape! I'll wait for my son to come. Whoa, ho, hoa!"

. . .

The Clown entered, calling, "Hilloa, loa!"

The shepherd asked, "What, are you near? Come see something to talk about when you're old. What's wrong?"

The Clown replied, "I've seen two incredible sights, by sea and by land! But now the sea is like the sky. You couldn't thrust a needle between them."

The shepherd urged, "Tell me, boy, what is it?"

The Clown explained, "The sea rages, it takes up the shore! But the most pitiful sight was the poor souls on the ship. Sometimes they were visible, sometimes not. The ship's mast seemed to bore into the moon, then it was swallowed by the waves. On land, a bear tore out a man's shoulder-bone. He cried for help, saying his name was Antigonus, a nobleman. The sea swallowed the ship, and the bear mocked the man, both roaring louder than the storm."

The shepherd, shocked, asked, "When did this happen?"

. . .

The Clown answered, "Just now. I haven't closed my eyes since. The men aren't yet cold in the water, nor the bear half done with the man."

The shepherd wished, "I wish I had been there to help the old man!"

The Clown replied, "You should have been by the ship to help it. Your charity would have been needed there."

The shepherd, overwhelmed, said, "Heavy matters! But look here, boy. Now bless yourself. You met with death, I with birth. Look at this sight! A baby, wrapped in a noble cloth! Take it up, open it. Let's see. I was told I'd be rich by the fairies. This must be a changeling. What's inside, boy?"

The Clown exclaimed, "You're a lucky old man! If your sins are forgiven, you'll live well. Gold! All gold!"

The shepherd marveled, "This is fairy gold, boy. Keep it secret. Let's go home. We are lucky, and secrecy will keep us so. Forget the sheep. Come, boy."

. . .

The Clown agreed, "You go home with your findings. I'll check if the bear has left anything of the gentleman. They're only vicious when hungry. If anything is left, I'll bury it."

The shepherd approved, "That's a good deed. If you can identify him, bring me to him."

The Clown promised, "I will, and you shall help bury him."

The shepherd concluded, "It's a lucky day, boy. Let's do good deeds on it."

They exited, carrying the baby and the gold.

ACT IV

SCENE 1

Time, the Chorus, stepped forward to address the audience.

"I, who bring joy and terror to all, who reveal both good and bad, who create and uncover errors, now take upon myself, in the name of Time, to use my wings. Do not hold it against me or my swift passage that I slide over sixteen years and leave the growth untried of that wide gap. It is within my power to defy laws and customs, planting and overwhelming them in a single hour. Let me pass as I have been, witnessing the ancient orders and the present, and making the glories of the present seem stale with my tale.

. . .

"Your patience allowing this, I turn my hourglass and let the scene grow as if you had slept through it. Imagine Leontes, still grieving from his jealousies, shutting himself away. Picture now, gentle spectators, fair Bohemia. Remember, I mentioned a son of the king's, whom I now name Florizel.

"And with speed, I bring to mind Perdita, now grown in grace and beauty, equal to any wonder. What follows for her, I will not predict. Let Time's news be known when it is brought forth.

"A shepherd's daughter and her story, which follows, is the argument of Time. Allow this if you have ever spent time worse than now; if never, may Time earnestly wish you never do."

With that, Time exited, setting the stage for the next chapter in the tale.

SCENE 2

At the palace of Polixenes in Bohemia, Polixenes and Camillo were engaged in a deep conversation.

Polixenes pleaded, "Please, good Camillo, don't insist on leaving. It's a pain to deny you anything, but granting this would feel like death."

Camillo replied, "It's been fifteen years since I saw my homeland. Though I've spent much time abroad, I wish to return and rest there. Besides, the penitent king, my master, has sent for me. He believes I might soothe his sorrows, and this thought spurs my departure."

. . .

Polixenes, struggling with the idea, said, "As you care for me, Camillo, don't erase your past services by leaving now. The need I have for you is because of your own good work. It would be better never to have had your help than to lose it now. You've created tasks that no one but you can manage. You must either stay to complete them or take away the benefit of your past services. If I haven't shown enough gratitude, I aim to be more thankful, enhancing our friendship. Speak no more of Sicilia, whose very name brings painful memories of my brother, the penitent and reconciled king. His loss of his queen and children is still fresh in my mind. Tell me, when did you last see Prince Florizel, my son? Kings are as unhappy when their children are not virtuous as they are when they lose them after proving their worth."

Camillo informed him, "Sir, it's been three days since I saw the prince. I don't know about his happier affairs, but I've noticed he's been keeping to himself and is less involved in his usual princely activities."

Polixenes, concerned, said, "I've observed that too, Camillo, and I've taken action. I've had people watch him, and they've reported that he often visits the house of a humble shepherd.

This man, they say, has suddenly become quite wealthy, beyond his neighbors' imagination."

Camillo added, "I've heard of such a man. He has a daughter of remarkable beauty and note, attracting attention beyond what one might expect from such a humble home."

Polixenes nodded, "Yes, that's what I've heard too. I fear it's the girl who draws our son there. You shall accompany me to this place. We will disguise ourselves and question the shepherd. From his simplicity, it shouldn't be hard to learn why our son visits him. Please, be my partner in this, and put aside thoughts of Sicilia for now."

Camillo agreed, "I willingly obey your command."

Polixenes, grateful, said, "My best Camillo! We must disguise ourselves."

With that, they exited, preparing to uncover the mystery of Florizel's visits.

SCENE 3

Autolycus walked along a road near the shepherd's cottage, singing cheerfully.

"When daffodils begin to peer,
  With heigh! the doxy over the dale,
  Why, then comes in the sweet o' the year;
  For the red blood reigns in the winter's pale.
  The white sheet bleaching on the hedge,
  With heigh! the sweet birds, O, how they sing!
  Doth set my pugging tooth on edge;
  For a quart of ale is a dish for a king.
  The lark, that tirra-lyra chants,
  With heigh! with heigh! the thrush and the jay,

Are summer songs for me and my aunts,
While we lie tumbling in the hay."

Autolycus stopped singing and spoke to himself. "I once served Prince Florizel and wore fine clothes, but now I am out of service. Should I mourn for that? No, the pale moon shines by night, and when I wander, I find my way. If tinkers can live and carry their bags, I can too. I sell trinkets and cheat people, but I avoid beating and hanging. As for the afterlife, I don't think about it. A prize! A prize!"

The Clown entered, counting money and mumbling to himself. "Let me see: every 'leven wether tods; every tod yields pound and odd shilling; fifteen hundred shorn. What comes the wool to?"

Autolycus, overhearing, thought to himself, "If my trap works, the fool is mine."

The Clown continued, "I cannot do it without counters. What am I to buy for our sheep-shearing feast? Three pounds of sugar, five pounds of currants, rice—what will my sister do with rice? But she is in charge of the feast and she's extravagant. She's made twenty-four nosegays for the shearers, good ones, but mostly for the middle and lower voices. One puritan among them sings psalms to horn-pipes. I need saffron for the warden pies; mace; dates—none of those, they're out of my list; nutmegs, seven; some ginger, which I can beg; four pounds of prunes and as many raisins."

Autolycus suddenly groaned and fell to the ground, pretending to be in pain. "O that ever I was born!"

The Clown noticed him. "In the name of me—"

Autolycus cried out, "O, help me, help me! Pull off these rags; and then, death, death!"

The Clown, feeling sorry, said, "Poor soul! You need more rags, not fewer."

Autolycus insisted, "O sir, these rags offend me more than the beatings I've received, which are many and severe."

. . .

The Clown lamented, "Alas, poor man! A million beatings is a lot."

Autolycus said, "I am robbed, sir, and beaten; my money and clothes taken, and these detestable rags put upon me."

The Clown asked, "By a horseman or a footman?"

Autolycus replied, "A footman, sweet sir, a footman."

The Clown observed, "By his clothes, he must be a footman. If this is a horseman's coat, it has seen very hot service. Let me help you up."

Autolycus pretended to be in great pain. "O, good sir, tenderly, O!"

The Clown continued, "Alas, poor soul!"

. . .

Autolycus moaned, "O, good sir, softly, good sir! I fear my shoulder-blade is out."

The Clown asked, "Can you stand?"

As he helped him, Autolycus picked the Clown's pocket. "Softly, dear sir; good sir, softly. You have done me a charitable office."

The Clown, feeling generous, said, "Do you need any money? I have a little for you."

Autolycus refused, "No, sweet sir; no, I beseech you, sir. I have a kinsman not far from here. I shall get money or anything I need there. Offer me no money; it breaks my heart."

The Clown asked, "What kind of man robbed you?"

Autolycus described, "A fellow I knew to go about with troll-my-dames; he was once a servant of the prince. I cannot tell for which of his virtues it was, but he was certainly whipped out of the court."

The Clown corrected, "His vices, you mean; there's no virtue whipped out of the court. They cherish virtue to make it stay there."

Autolycus agreed, "Vices, I meant, sir. I know this man well. He has been an ape-bearer, a process-server, a bailiff, then married a tinker's wife near my land. After many knavish professions, he settled as a rogue. Some call him Autolycus."

The Clown cursed, "Out upon him! A thief! He haunts wakes, fairs, and bear-baitings."

Autolycus confirmed, "Very true, sir. He's the rogue who put me in these clothes."

The Clown commented, "Not a more cowardly rogue in all Bohemia. If you had looked fierce and spit at him, he'd have run."

. . .

Autolycus confessed, "I must admit, sir, I am no fighter. I am false-hearted that way; and he knew it."

The Clown asked, "How do you feel now?"

Autolycus replied, "Much better, sweet sir; I can stand and walk. I will leave you and head towards my kinsman's."

The Clown offered, "Shall I walk with you?"

Autolycus declined, "No, good sir; no, sweet sir."

The Clown said farewell, "Then fare thee well. I must buy spices for our sheep-shearing."

Autolycus wished him well, "Prosper you, sweet sir!"

As the Clown exited, Autolycus smiled to himself, "Your purse is not hot enough to purchase your spice. I'll be at your sheep-shearing too. If I don't make this cheat bring out more and turn the shearers into sheep, let my name be stricken from the book of virtue!"

Singing again, he walked off.

"Jog on, jog on, the foot-path way,
    And merrily hent the stile-a:
    A merry heart goes all the day,
    Your sad tires in a mile-a."

Autolycus exited, planning his next scheme.

SCENE 4

At the shepherd's cottage, Florizel and Perdita stood together, both disguised for the festive occasion.

Florizel admired her, saying, "These unusual clothes give you new life. You look like Flora, the goddess of flowers, presiding over April. This sheep-shearing is like a gathering of minor gods, and you are their queen."

Perdita responded, "Sir, my gracious lord, it doesn't become me to criticize your extremes. Pardon me for even mentioning them. You, the esteemed prince, are dressed like a common shepherd, while I, a lowly maid, am dressed like a goddess. But our feasts always have folly, and the diners are accustomed to it. Otherwise, I would blush to see you so attired, as if you were a mirror reflecting me."

Florizel said, "I bless the day when my good falcon flew across your father's land."

Perdita replied, "May the gods grant you cause to be happy! The difference in our stations fills me with dread. Your greatness has never known fear, but I tremble to think your father might pass this way by accident, as you did. O, the Fates! How would he react to see his noble son so humbly dressed? What would he say? How could I, in these borrowed clothes, face his stern gaze?"

Florizel reassured her, "Don't worry about anything but joy. The gods themselves have taken on humble forms for love. Jupiter became a bull, Neptune a ram, and Apollo a shepherd, just as I am now. Their transformations were never for a beauty rarer than yours, nor in such a chaste manner. My desires do not outstrip my honor, nor do my lusts burn hotter than my faith."

. . .

Perdita warned, "But, sir, your resolve cannot hold when opposed by the king's power. You must either change your purpose, or I my life."

Florizel declared, "Dearest Perdita, do not darken the joy of the feast with such thoughts. I will be yours, or not my father's son. I cannot be mine own, nor anyone else's, if I am not yours. I am constant in this, though destiny says no. Be merry, gentle; dismiss these thoughts with anything else you see. Your guests are coming. Lift up your countenance as if it were the day of our promised wedding."

Perdita prayed, "O lady Fortune, be favorable!"

Florizel pointed out, "See, your guests approach. Greet them with joy, and let us be red with mirth."

The shepherd, Clown, Mopsa, Dorcas, and others entered, with Polixenes and Camillo disguised among them.

The shepherd chided, "Fie, daughter! When my old wife lived, she took care of everything on this day. She was both cook and server, welcomed all, served all, sang and danced, moving from one end of the table to the other. Her face was flushed with labor and drink. You are withdrawn, acting like a guest instead of the hostess. Please, welcome these unknown friends; it will make us better friends. Show yourself as the mistress of the feast. Come, bid us welcome to your sheep-shearing, as your good flock shall prosper."

Perdita welcomed the disguised Polixenes and Camillo, saying, "Sir, welcome. It is my father's will that I take on the role of hostess today. Welcome, sir." She asked Dorcas for flowers, saying, "Give me those flowers, Dorcas. Reverend sirs, here are rosemary and rue for you. They keep their appearance and fragrance all winter. Grace and remembrance to you both, and welcome to our shearing!"

Polixenes remarked, "Shepherdess, you are a fair one and well fit our ages with flowers of winter."

Perdita responded, "Sir, the year is growing old, not yet summer's end nor winter's birth. The fairest flowers now are carnations and streaked gillyflowers, which some call nature's bastards. Our rustic garden is barren of them, and I care not to get slips of them."

. . .

Polixenes asked, "Why do you neglect them, gentle maiden?"

Perdita explained, "I have heard that there is an art in their piedness that competes with nature."

Polixenes countered, "Say there is such an art, yet nature is made better by no means but what nature makes. Art that adds to nature is also made by nature. We marry a gentler scion to the wildest stock and make a baser kind noble by grafting. This art improves nature, changes it, but the art itself is nature."

Perdita conceded, "So it is."

Polixenes encouraged, "Then make your garden rich in gillyflowers and do not call them bastards."

Perdita firmly said, "I will not plant a single slip of them. I would no more plant them than if I were painted and wanted this youth to say it was well and therefore desire to breed by me. Here are flowers for you; hot lavender, mints, savory, marjoram; the marigold, which goes to bed with the sun and rises weeping with him. These are flowers of midsummer, and I think they are given to men of middle age. You're very welcome."

Camillo admired, "I should leave grazing if I were of your flock and live only by gazing."

Perdita playfully responded, "Out, alas! You'd grow so lean that January's blasts would blow through you. Now, my fairest friend, I wish I had spring flowers to suit your time of day. Daffodils, that come before the swallow dares and take the winds of March with beauty; violets, sweeter than Juno's eyes or Cytherea's breath; pale primroses that die unmarried; bold oxlips and the crown imperial; lilies of all kinds. O, I lack these to make garlands for you, my sweet friend, to strew over and over!"

Florizel asked, "What, like a corpse?"

Perdita corrected him, "No, like a bank for love to lie and play on. Not like a corpse; or if so, not to be buried, but alive and in my arms. Come, take your flowers. I feel as if I play a part in Whitsun pastorals. This robe changes my disposition."

Florizel praised, "What you do improves everything. When you speak, I'd have you do it always; when you sing, I'd have you buy and sell, give alms, pray, and manage affairs in song. When you dance, I wish you were like the sea waves, moving eternally, and doing nothing else. Each of your actions crowns the present deed, making all your acts royal."

Perdita, feeling overwhelmed, said, "O Doricles, your praises are too much. But your youth and the true blood that shines through it show you are an unstained shepherd. I might fear you woo me falsely if I did not trust you."

Florizel assured her, "You have as little reason to fear as I have intention to deceive. But come, let's dance. Your hand, my Perdita, like turtles that never part."

Perdita agreed, "I'll swear for them."

. . .

Polixenes, watching them, remarked, "This is the prettiest low-born lass that ever ran on the green-sward. Everything she does or seems smacks of something greater than herself, too noble for this place."

Camillo, observing Perdita's interaction with Florizel, noted, "He tells her something that makes her blush. Truly, she is the queen of curds and cream."

The Clown, eager to continue the festivities, called out, "Come on, strike up the music!"

Dorcas teased, "Mopsa must be your mistress, Clown. She should have some garlic to improve her kisses!"

Mopsa, taken aback, responded, "Now, that's timely!"

The Clown interrupted, "Not a word, not a word; we must maintain our manners. Come, strike up the music!"

Music began, and shepherds and shepherdesses danced.

. . .

A servant rushed in, exclaiming, "O master, if you heard the pedlar at the door, you'd never dance again to a tabor and pipe; even the bagpipe wouldn't move you. He sings tunes faster than you can count money; it's as if he eats ballads and everyone's ears grow to his tunes."

The Clown, excited, said, "He couldn't have come at a better time. Bring him in. I love a ballad, whether it's a sad story told merrily or a very pleasant thing sung lamentably."

The Servant added, "He has songs for everyone, just like a milliner fits customers with gloves. He has the prettiest love-songs for maids, free of bawdiness, which is rare. With delicate refrains like 'jump her and thump her,' he turns potential mischief into harmless fun."

Polixenes remarked, "This is a brave fellow."

The Clown agreed, "Indeed, he sounds like an admirable fellow. Does he have any unbraided wares?"

. . .

The Servant replied, "He has ribbons of every color in the rainbow, more points than all the lawyers in Bohemia could handle, inkles, caddisses, cambrics, lawns. He sings about them as if they were gods or goddesses. You'd think a smock was a she-angel, he chants so sweetly about it."

The Clown said, "Bring him in, and let him approach singing."

Perdita, cautious, advised, "Warn him not to use any scurrilous words in his songs."

The Servant exited to fetch the pedlar, and the Clown told Perdita, "These pedlars have more in them than you might think, sister."

Perdita agreed, "Yes, good brother, they do."

Autolycus entered, singing:

"Lawn as white as driven snow;
    Cyprus black as e'er was crow;

Gloves as sweet as damask roses;
Masks for faces and for noses;
Bugle bracelet, necklace amber,
Perfume for a lady's chamber;
Golden quoifs and stomachers,
For my lads to give their dears:
Pins and poking-sticks of steel,
What maids lack from head to heel:
Come buy of me, come; come buy, come buy;
Buy lads, or else your lasses cry: Come buy."

The Clown, charmed by the song, said, "If I weren't in love with Mopsa, you wouldn't get any money from me. But since I'm enthralled, I'll have to buy some ribbons and gloves."

Mopsa chimed in, "I was promised these for the feast, and they haven't come too late."

Dorcas added, "He promised you more than that, unless there are liars."

Mopsa replied, "He has given you everything he promised. Maybe he's given you more, which would shame you to return."

. . .

The Clown admonished, "Is there no manners left among maids? Will they gossip in front of our guests? Save such talk for milking-time or when going to bed. Now, silence!"

Mopsa said, "I've finished. Come, you promised me a tawdry-lace and sweet gloves."

The Clown explained, "Didn't I tell you I was tricked on the way and lost all my money?"

Autolycus interjected, "Indeed, sir, there are swindlers about; one must be wary."

The Clown reassured, "Fear not, man, you won't lose anything here."

Autolycus said, "I hope so, sir; for I have many valuable items with me."

The Clown asked, "What do you have here? Ballads?"

. . .

Mopsa eagerly said, "Please, buy some. I love a ballad in print, for then we know they are true."

Autolycus offered, "Here's one to a very doleful tune, about a usurer's wife who gave birth to twenty money-bags at once and longed to eat adders' heads and toads."

Mopsa asked, "Is it true, do you think?"

Autolycus assured, "Very true, and only a month old."

Dorcas prayed, "Bless me from marrying a usurer!"

Autolycus added, "Here's the midwife's name, Mistress Taleporter, and five or six honest wives who were present. Why should I carry lies?"

Mopsa urged, "Please, buy it."

. . .

The Clown said, "Set it aside; let's see more ballads first. We'll buy other things later."

Autolycus continued, "Here's another ballad about a fish that appeared on the coast on the eighty-fourth of April, forty thousand fathoms above water. It sang this ballad against the hard hearts of maids. It was thought to be a woman turned into a fish for refusing to love. The ballad is very pitiful and true."

Dorcas asked, "Is it true too, do you think?"

Autolycus affirmed, "Five justices' hands on it, and more witnesses than my pack can hold."

The Clown said, "Set that one aside too; another."

Autolycus introduced, "This is a merry ballad, but very pretty."

. . .

Mopsa requested, "Let's have some merry ones."

Autolycus complied, "This one is very merry and goes to the tune of 'Two maids wooing a man.' Almost every maid westward sings it. It's popular, I assure you."

Mopsa announced, "We can both sing it. If you'll join us, we'll sing it in three parts."

Dorcas added, "We learned the tune a month ago."

Autolycus agreed, "I can join. It's my trade. Let's sing."

They began to sing:

"Get you hence, for I must go
    Where it fits not you to know."

Dorcas and Mopsa asked in unison, "Whither? O, whither?"

. . .

Autolycus continued:

"It becomes thy oath full well,
    Thou to me thy secrets tell."

Dorcas and Mopsa repeated, "Me too, let me go thither."

Autolycus replied:
    "Or thou goest to the orange or mill.
    If to either, thou dost ill."

Dorcas and Mopsa pressed, "What, neither? Neither?"
    Autolycus confirmed, "Neither."

Dorcas lamented, "Thou hast sworn my love to be."
    Mopsa added, "Thou hast sworn it more to me. Then whither goest? Say, whither?"

The Clown, deciding to save the rest of the song for later, said, "We'll have this song out later by ourselves. My father and the gentlemen are in serious talk, and we don't want to trouble them. Come, bring your pack. I'll buy for you both. Pedlar, let us have the first choice. Follow me, girls."

As the Clown exited with Dorcas and Mopsa, Autolycus followed, singing:

"Will you buy any tape,
    Or lace for your cape,
    My dainty duck, my dear-a?
    Any silk, any thread,
    Any toys for your head,
    Of the new'st and finest, finest wear-a?
    Come to the pedlar;
    Money's a medler.
    That doth utter all men's ware-a."

Just then, the servant returned, announcing, "Master, there are three carters, three shepherds, three neat-herds, and three swine-herds who have made themselves all men of hair. They call themselves Saltiers, and they have a dance which the girls call a jumble of gambols because they aren't in it. But the men believe that if it's not too rough for those who know little beyond bowling, it will please greatly."

. . .

The Shepherd, tired of the commotion, said, "Away! We'll have none of it. There's been too much rustic foolery already. I know, sir, we weary you."

Polixenes, however, replied, "You weary those who refresh us. Pray, let us see these twelve herdsmen."

The Servant added, "One of them claims to have danced before the king, and not the worst of them can jump twelve and a half feet by measure."

The Shepherd relented, "Stop your prattling. Since these good men are pleased, let them come in, but quickly now."

The Servant exited to fetch the dancers, and soon a group of twelve Satyrs entered and performed their dance.

Polixenes, speaking aside to Camillo, remarked, "O father, you'll know more about that later. It's time to separate them. This young man speaks too much."

. . .

Turning to Florizel, Polixenes asked, "How now, fair shepherd! Your heart seems full of something that takes your mind from feasting. When I was young and in love like you, I would have bought every trinket from the pedlar for my lady. But you let him go without buying anything. If your lass interprets this as a lack of love or generosity, you would be hard-pressed to explain otherwise if you care about keeping her."

Florizel answered, "Old sir, she prizes not such trifles as these. The gifts she expects from me are already locked in my heart, which I have given but not yet delivered. O, hear me breathe my life before this ancient sir, who seems to have loved before! I take thy hand, this hand, as soft as dove's down and as white as snow."

Polixenes inquired, "What follows this? How prettily the young swain seems to wash the hand that was fair before! But continue your declaration; let me hear what you profess."

Florizel replied, "Do, and be witness to it."

. . .

Polixenes asked, "And this my neighbor too?"

Florizel affirmed, "And he, and more than he, and men, the earth, the heavens, and all. If I were crowned the most imperial monarch, the fairest youth, with more force and knowledge than any man, I would not prize them without her love. I would use them all for her, commend them to her service, or condemn them to their own ruin."

Polixenes commented, "Fairly offered."

Camillo noted, "This shows a sincere affection."

The Shepherd asked Perdita, "But, my daughter, do you feel the same for him?"

Perdita replied, "I cannot speak as well, nor mean better. By the pattern of my thoughts, I judge his purity."

The Shepherd declared, "Take hands, a bargain! And, friends

unknown, bear witness. I give my daughter to him and will make her portion equal to his."

Florizel added, "That must be in the virtue of your daughter. One being dead, I shall have more than you can dream of yet. Enough then for your wonder. But come, let us seal our contract before these witnesses."

The Shepherd invited, "Come, your hand; and, daughter, yours."

Polixenes interrupted, "Soft, swain, a while, I beseech you. Do you have a father?"

Florizel replied, "I do. But what of him?"

Polixenes asked, "Does he know of this?"

Florizel answered, "He neither does nor shall."

. . .

Polixenes reasoned, "It seems to me that a father at his son's wedding is a guest who best fits the table. Is your father unable to handle reasonable affairs? Is he senile or bedridden?"

Florizel responded, "No, good sir. He is healthy and strong for his age."

Polixenes admonished, "By my white beard, you wrong him by not involving him in this decision. It's reasonable for a son to choose a wife, but also reasonable for a father, whose joy is in his posterity, to be consulted."

Florizel yielded, "I understand, but for reasons not fit for you to know, I will not inform my father of this matter."

Polixenes insisted, "Let him know."

Florizel refused, "He shall not."

. . .

Polixenes pleaded, "Prithee, let him."

Florizel stood firm, "No, he must not."

The Shepherd encouraged, "Let him know, my son. He need not grieve over your choice."

Florizel remained resolute, "Come, come, he must not. Mark our contract."

Polixenes revealed himself, "Mark your divorce, young sir. Whom son I dare not call; thou art too base to be acknowledged. Thou, a sceptre's heir, who thus affects a sheep-hook! Thou old traitor, I'm sorry that by hanging thee, I can only shorten thy life by a week. And thou, fresh piece of excellent witchcraft, who must know the royal fool thou copes with--"

The Shepherd, shocked, exclaimed, "O, my heart!"

Polixenes continued, "I'll have thy beauty scratched with briers and made more homely than thy state. And you, boy, if

I ever know you sigh for her again, you shall be barred from succession and not considered our kin. Follow us to the court. Thou churl, though full of our displeasure, we free thee from the death blow this time. But if you, Perdita, ever let him in your house again, I will devise a death as cruel as you are tender."

Polixenes exited, leaving Perdita and Florizel devastated.

Perdita, heartbroken, said, "Even here, undone! I was not much afraid; I almost spoke out. The same sun that shines on his court looks on our cottage. Will you leave now? I told you this would happen. Take care of your own state. This dream is over for me. I will return to milking my ewes and weeping."

Camillo urged the Shepherd, "Why, how now, father! Speak before you die."

The Shepherd, despairing, said, "I cannot speak, nor think, nor dare to know what I know. O sir, you have undone a man of eighty-three, who thought to die in peace. But now, I must face a hangman's shroud. O cursed wretch, that knew this was the prince and mingled faith with him! Undone, undone! If I might die within this hour, I have lived long enough."

He exited, leaving Florizel to face the consequences.

Florizel asked, "Why look you so upon me? I am but sorry, not afraid. Delayed, but unchanged. What I was, I am, striving harder for being pulled back."

Camillo, wise and understanding, advised Florizel, "Gracious my lord, you know your father's temper. He will not tolerate any speech now, nor endure your sight. Wait until his fury settles before you approach him."

Florizel replied, "I do not intend to see him. What do you think, Camillo?"

Perdita, concerned, added, "How often have I told you it would be like this! How often did I say that my dignity would last only until it was known!"

. . .

Florizel, determined, said, "It cannot fail unless I violate my faith. Let nature crush the earth together if it must. Look up, Perdita. Father, wipe me from your succession; I am heir to my own affection."

Camillo warned, "Be advised."

Florizel replied, "I am advised by my heart. If my reason follows, then I have reason. If not, I welcome madness, which pleases my senses better."

Camillo said, "This is desperate, sir."

Florizel declared, "Call it desperate if you will; it fulfills my vow. I must remain honest. Camillo, not for Bohemia, nor for all the riches of the world, will I break my oath to my beloved. Therefore, I ask you, as my father's honored friend, to counsel him in my absence. Tell him that I have set sail with her, and a ship conveniently waits nearby, though not prepared for this. Our course is no concern of yours."

. . .

Camillo, concerned, exclaimed, "O my lord! I wish your spirit were easier for advice or stronger for your needs."

Florizel turned to Perdita, "Hark, Perdita. I'll hear you by and by."

Camillo thought to himself, "He is determined to flee. If I can turn this to my advantage, save him from danger, gain his love and honor, and see Sicilia and my old master again, it would be a blessing."

Florizel returned, saying, "Good Camillo, I am so busy with urgent matters that I must dispense with formalities."

Camillo replied, "Sir, I think you have heard of my loyal service and love for your father?"

Florizel answered, "You have deserved much praise. It is my father's habit to speak highly of your deeds and to repay them."

. . .

Camillo suggested, "If you trust my loyalty to the king and to you, follow my advice. If you can alter your plans, I will guide you to a place where you can safely marry your beloved. I will strive to calm your father's anger and bring him to accept your union."

Florizel asked, "How, Camillo? If you can achieve this, I will trust you implicitly."

Camillo asked, "Have you chosen a destination?"

Florizel replied, "Not yet. We are at the mercy of chance and will go wherever fate leads."

Camillo proposed, "Then listen. If you are determined to flee, head to Sicilia. Present yourself and your princess to Leontes. She will be dressed as befits your bride. I foresee Leontes welcoming you with open arms, asking for your father's forgiveness, and embracing your princess. He will divide himself between his past unkindness and present kindness."

. . .

Florizel asked, "What reason shall I give for my visit?"

Camillo answered, "Say that your father sent you to greet him and offer comfort. I will write down what you should say to make it seem as though you speak your father's very heart."

Florizel agreed, "I am bound to you. There is promise in this plan."

Camillo continued, "This is more hopeful than wandering aimlessly, facing certain miseries. Prosperity strengthens love, while affliction weakens it."

Perdita remarked, "I believe affliction may affect the face but not the mind."

Camillo responded, "Indeed. There shall not be another born in your father's house for seven years as exceptional as you."

Florizel, proud of Perdita, said, "My good Camillo, she is advanced in her qualities, beyond her noble birth."

Camillo praised, "I cannot say she lacks instruction, for she seems a master to most who teach."

Perdita, modest, said, "Your pardon, sir. I blush with thanks."

Florizel, tenderly, called her, "My prettiest Perdita! But O, the thorns we stand upon! Camillo, savior of my father, now of me, healer of our house, what shall we do? We are not equipped like Bohemia's son, nor shall we appear as such in Sicilia."

Camillo reassured Florizel, "My lord, fear none of this. You know my fortunes lie in Sicilia, and I will ensure you are royally appointed, as if the scene were my own. Let me speak a word with you."

As they spoke aside, Autolycus reentered, chuckling, "Ha, ha! What a fool honesty is, and trust, his brother, is a simpleton! I've sold all my trinkets, not a counterfeit stone, ribbon, or brooch left. They thronged to buy as if my goods were blessed. The clown, infatuated with the wenches' song, didn't move until he had both tune and words. While everyone was distracted, I picked and cut their purses. Had the old man not scared them off with his outcry, I wouldn't have left a single purse alive."

Camillo, Florizel, and Perdita came forward. Camillo said, "My letters will clear any doubt when you arrive."

Florizel added, "And the letters you'll procure from King Leontes will satisfy your father."

Perdita, hopeful, said, "Happy be you! Everything you say sounds fair."

Camillo, noticing Autolycus, said, "Who have we here? We'll make use of this. Nothing should be overlooked."

Autolycus, fearing he had been overheard, thought, "If they heard me, I'm done for."

Camillo called out, "How now, good fellow! Why do you shake? Fear not; there's no harm intended."

Autolycus replied, "I am a poor fellow, sir."

Camillo responded, "Remain so; no one will steal that from you. But we need to make an exchange. Disrobe instantly and change garments with this gentleman. There's a necessity in it."

Autolycus, pretending to resist, said, "I am a poor fellow, sir. I know you well enough."

Camillo insisted, "Nay, prithee, dispatch. The gentleman is half undressed already."

Autolycus, suspecting a trick, asked, "Are you in earnest, sir?"

Florizel urged, "Dispatch, I prithee."

Autolycus reluctantly agreed, "Indeed, I have had earnest, but I cannot take it with a clear conscience."

Camillo commanded, "Unbuckle, unbuckle."

As Florizel and Autolycus exchanged garments, Camillo instructed Perdita, "You must disguise yourself. Take your sweetheart's hat, muffle your face, and change your appearance as best as you can. We must get you to the ship unnoticed."

Perdita agreed, "I see I must play my part."

Camillo nodded, "No remedy. Have you done?"

Florizel, fully disguised, said, "If I met my father now, he would not recognize me."

Camillo gave Perdita the hat, saying, "You shall have no hat. Come, lady, come. Farewell, my friend."

Autolycus responded, "Adieu, sir."

Florizel, anxious, said, "O Perdita, what have we forgotten? Pray, a word."

Camillo, aside, thought, "Next, I'll inform the king of this escape and their destination. I hope to persuade him to follow, allowing me to see Sicilia again."

Florizel, determined, said, "Fortune speed us! Let's head to the seaside."

Camillo agreed, "The swifter the better."

As they exited, Autolycus mused, "I understand the business. A quick ear, a sharp eye, and a nimble hand are necessary for a cut-purse. This is the time when the unjust thrive. What an exchange this has been!"

Re-entering, the Clown and Shepherd approached, discussing their plan to tell the king everything.

Clown said, "See, what a man you are now! There's no other way but to tell the king she's a changeling and not your flesh and blood."

Shepherd replied, "Nay, but hear me."

Clown insisted, "Nay, but hear me. She being none of your flesh and blood, you are not to be punished by the king. Show him the things you found about her, and let the law whistle."

Shepherd decided, "I will tell the king everything, including his son's pranks."

Clown added, "Indeed, brother-in-law was the farthest off you could have been to him."

Autolycus, aside, thought, "Very wisely, puppies!"

Shepherd concluded, "Let's go to the king. This will make him scratch his beard."

Autolycus, aside, worried, "I wonder what this complaint might mean for my master's flight."

Clown hoped, "Pray he is at the palace."

Autolycus, pretending honesty, said, "Though I am not naturally honest, sometimes I am by chance. Let me pocket my pedlar's disguise. How now, rustics! Where are you bound?"

Shepherd answered, "To the palace, sir."

Autolycus inquired, "Your affairs there? What is in that bundle?"

Clown, wary, said, "We are plain fellows, sir."

Autolycus, dismissing their modesty, said, "Nonsense! Speak up."

Shepherd, confused, asked, "Are you a courtier, sir?"

Autolycus proudly replied, "Indeed, I am. Open your business to me."

Shepherd hesitated, "My business is to the king."

Autolycus asked, "What advocate do you have?"

Shepherd replied, "None, sir."

Clown whispered, "Say you have none."

Shepherd admitted, "None, sir."

. . .

Autolycus, relishing his role, said, "Blessed are we not simple men! Tell me your business with the king, and I will bring you to him."

Shepherd, seeing a chance, said, "Sir, we have important news. Here is gold for your help."

Autolycus agreed, "Well, give me the gold. I will take you to the king."

Clown, hopeful, said, "We must tell him everything. Sir, I will give you as much as this old man when the business is done."

Autolycus, seeing an opportunity, said, "I will trust you. Walk toward the seaside. I will follow."

Clown, grateful, said, "We are blessed in this man."

Shepherd added, "Let's go as he bids."

. . .

As they left, Autolycus planned, "If I had a mind to be honest, Fortune would not allow it. I am courted by gold and a chance to do my master good. I will present these fools to him."

ACT V

SCENE 1

In a room in Leontes' palace, Leontes sat with Cleomenes, Dion, Paulina, and several servants.

Cleomenes said, "Sir, you have done enough, and shown saint-like sorrow. You have redeemed any faults and paid more penitence than trespass. Do as the heavens have done and forgive yourself."

Leontes responded, "While I remember her and her virtues, I cannot forget my blemishes in them. I did myself such wrong that it has made my kingdom heirless and destroyed the sweetest companion a man ever had."

. . .

Paulina agreed, "True, too true, my lord. Even if you married every woman in the world and took the best parts to make a perfect woman, she whom you killed would still be unparalleled."

Leontes sighed, "I think so. I killed her! I did so. But it's painful to hear you say it. Please say it less often."

Cleomenes added, "Not at all, good lady. You might have spoken a thousand things that would have been more beneficial and kind."

Paulina insisted, "You are one of those who would have him wed again."

Dion replied, "If you would not, you pity not the state nor the memory of his most sovereign name. Consider the dangers of his highness' lack of issue that may fall upon his kingdom. What could be more holy than to rejoice that the former queen is well? What could be holier than to bless the bed of majesty again for comfort and future good?"

. . .

Paulina protested, "There is none worthy, respecting her that's gone. Besides, the gods will fulfill their secret purposes. Hasn't Apollo's oracle said that King Leontes shall not have an heir till his lost child is found? To counsel against that is to oppose the heavens."

Turning to Leontes, she continued, "Care not for issue; the crown will find an heir. Great Alexander left his to the worthiest. So, his successor was the best."

Leontes said, "Good Paulina, who has the memory of Hermione, I know, in honor, O, that I had followed your counsel! Even now, I might have looked upon my queen's eyes, taken treasure from her lips--"

Paulina interrupted, "And left them more rich for what they yielded."

Leontes admitted, "You speak the truth. No more such wives; therefore, no wife. A worse wife, better treated, would make her sainted spirit return to possess her corpse and appear on this stage, asking, 'Why to me?'"

Paulina declared, "Had she such power, she had just cause."

Leontes agreed, "She had, and would urge me to murder her I married."

Paulina continued, "I should too. Were I her ghost, I'd tell you to mark her eye and ask what dull part in it you chose her for; then I'd shriek, making your ears split, and say, 'Remember mine.'"

Leontes sighed, "Stars, stars, and all other eyes dead coals! Fear no wife, Paulina; I'll have no wife."

Paulina asked, "Will you swear never to marry but by my leave?"

Leontes responded, "Never, Paulina; so be my spirit blessed!"

. . .

Paulina said, "Then, good lords, bear witness to his oath."

Cleomenes suggested, "You tempt him too much."

Paulina added, "Unless another, as like Hermione as her picture, stands before his eye."

Cleomenes interjected, "Good madam--"

Paulina replied, "I have done. Yet, if my lord will marry, give me the office to choose you a queen. She shall not be as young as your former but such that Hermione's ghost would rejoice to see her in your arms."

Leontes vowed, "My true Paulina, we shall not marry till you bid us."

Paulina insisted, "That shall be when your first queen breathes again; never till then."

. . .

A gentleman entered and announced, "One who calls himself Prince Florizel, son of Polixenes, with his princess, the fairest I have ever seen, desires access to your presence."

Leontes inquired, "What brings him here? He doesn't come like his father's greatness. His sudden approach tells us it's not a planned visit. What train?"

The Gentleman answered, "But few, and those mean."

Leontes asked, "His princess, say you, with him?"

The Gentleman affirmed, "Yes, the most peerless piece of earth the sun has ever shone on."

Paulina exclaimed, "O Hermione, as every present time boasts itself above the past, so must your grave give way to what's seen now! Sir, you yourself have said and written so. But your writing now is colder than that theme, 'She had not been, nor was not to be equalled;' thus your verse once flowed with her beauty. It's diminished now to say you have seen a better."

. . .

The Gentleman apologized, "Pardon, madam: I had almost forgotten one; your pardon. The other, when she has obtained your eye, will have your tongue too. This is a creature who, if she began a sect, might quench the zeal of all other followers, making proselytes of those she bid follow."

Paulina asked, "How! Not women?"

The Gentleman explained, "Women will love her, as she is a woman more worth than any man; men, because she is the rarest of all women."

Leontes instructed, "Go, Cleomenes, bring them to us. Still, it's strange he should come upon us like this."

Paulina reflected, "Had our prince, jewel of children, seen this hour, he would have matched well with this lord: there was less than a month between their births."

. . .

Leontes pleaded, "No more; cease; you know he dies to me again when talked of. They are here."

Cleomenes reentered with Florizel and Perdita. Leontes greeted them, "Your mother was true to wedlock, prince; she imprinted your royal father in you. Were I but twenty-one, I would call you brother. Most dearly welcome! And your fair princess--goddess!--O, alas! I lost a couple that might have stood begetting wonder like you. All my own folly. But welcome! And your fair princess--goddess!--O, alas! I lost a couple that might have stood begetting wonder as you do. And then I lost--all mine own folly--the company of your brave father. Though bearing misery, I wish to see him once more."

Florizel said, "By his command, I have come to Sicilia to bring you all greetings from him. If not for infirmity, he would have crossed lands and waters to see you himself."

Leontes exclaimed, "O my brother, good gentleman! The wrongs I have done you stir afresh within me. These kind offices are as interpreters of my neglect. Welcome, as is the spring to the earth. Did he expose this paragon to the rough seas to greet a man unworthy of her?"

. . .

Florizel explained, "She came from Libya."

Leontes inquired, "Where the warlike Smalus is feared and loved?"

Florizel replied, "Most royal sir, from thence. His tears proclaimed his parting with her. A friendly south wind brought us here to execute my father's charge."

Leontes said, "The gods purge all infection from our air while you are here! You have a holy father, a graceful gentleman. Against him, I have sinned. For which the heavens, taking angry note, have left me issueless. Your father is blessed with you, worthy of his goodness. What might I have been, could I look on such goodly things as you!"

A Lord entered and reported, "Most noble sir, Bohemia greets you and desires you to apprehend his son, who has fled with a shepherd's daughter."

. . .

Leontes asked, "Where's Bohemia?"

The Lord answered, "Here in your city. To your court, he hastened, in pursuit of this couple. He met the father of this lady and her brother."

Florizel exclaimed, "Camillo has betrayed me; his honor and honesty have endured all weathers until now."

The Lord confirmed, "Camillo is with the king your father. I spoke with him; he has these poor men in question. Bohemia stops his ears and threatens them with various deaths."

Perdita lamented, "O my poor father! The heaven sets spies upon us, will not have our contract celebrated."

Leontes asked, "You are married?"

Florizel replied, "We are not, sir, nor are we like to be."

. . .

Leontes asked, "Is this the daughter of a king?"

Florizel said, "She is, when once she is my wife."

Leontes observed, "Your father's speed shows that 'once' will come slowly. I am sorry you have broken from his liking, and as sorry your choice is not so rich in worth as beauty."

Florizel reassured Perdita, "Dear, look up. Fortune has no power to change our loves. Beseech you, sir, remember when you owed no more to time than I do now. With thoughts of such affections, be my advocate."

Leontes said, "I would beg your precious mistress, which he counts a trifle."

Paulina cautioned, "Sir, your eye has too much youth. Not a month before your queen died, she was more worth such gazes than what you look on now."

Leontes admitted, "I thought of her in these looks. But

. . .

your petition is yet unanswered. I will to your father. Your honor not overthrown by your desires, I am friend to them and you. Follow me and mark what way I make. Come, good my lord."

SCENE 2

Outside Leontes' palace, Autolycus spoke with a Gentleman.

Autolycus asked, "Were you present at this revelation?"

The Gentleman replied, "I was there when the bundle was opened. The old shepherd explained how he found it. After some initial amazement, we were all commanded out of the chamber. I heard the shepherd say he found the child."

. . .

Autolycus said, "I would love to know the outcome."

The Gentleman continued, "I can only tell you bits and pieces. The king and Camillo were astounded. Their silent reactions spoke volumes. It looked like they had heard of a world being saved or destroyed. A deep wonder filled the room. The wisest observer wouldn't know if the news brought joy or sorrow, but it was definitely extreme."

Another Gentleman arrived. "What's the news, Rogero?"

Rogero said, "Bonfires everywhere! The oracle is fulfilled; the king's daughter is found. There's so much wonder that ballad-makers can't keep up."

A third Gentleman entered. "Paulina's steward can tell you more. How goes it, sir? The news sounds like an old tale, making the truth suspicious. Has the king found his heir?"

The Steward confirmed, "It's true, as the circumstances reveal. The proof is undeniable: the queen's mantle, her jewel, Antigonus's letters, the princess's resemblance to her mother, and her noble nature. Did you see the meeting of the two kings?"

The second Gentleman said, "No."

The Steward replied, "You missed an unforgettable sight. One joy crowned another. The kings' joy was so great that it seemed sorrow wept to leave them. Our king was overjoyed at finding his daughter, then cried out about her mother, asked Bohemia for forgiveness, and embraced his son-in-law. The old shepherd stood by, witnessing this historic moment. The encounter was beyond description."

The second Gentleman asked, "What happened to Antigonus, who carried away the child?"

The Steward explained, "An old tale again. Antigonus was torn to pieces by a bear. The shepherd's son witnessed it and has Antigonus's handkerchief and rings, which Paulina recognized."

. . .

The first Gentleman asked, "What happened to his ship and followers?"

The Steward said, "Wrecked at the same time as Antigonus's death. All the instruments that exposed the child were lost when the child was found. Paulina, torn between joy and sorrow, embraced the princess as if to never let her go."

The first Gentleman noted, "The dignity of this act deserved the audience of kings and princes."

The Steward added, "One touching moment was when the king confessed and lamented the queen's death. His daughter's grief was so intense that she seemed to bleed tears. Everyone was deeply moved."

The first Gentleman asked, "Are they back at court?"

The Steward said, "No, they went to see the queen's statue, kept by Paulina. It's an extraordinary piece by Julio Romano. They intend to stay there."

. . .

The second Gentleman remarked, "I thought she had something important there. Shall we join them?"

The first Gentleman agreed, "Who would miss this? Every moment brings new grace. Let's go."

The Gentlemen exited.

Autolycus, now alone, mused, "Had I not my past life's flaws, I'd be promoted. I brought the old man and his son aboard the prince's ship. They spoke of a bundle, but the prince, distracted by the shepherd's daughter, ignored it. The storm hid the secret. But it's all the same to me. Even if I had revealed it, it wouldn't have helped my reputation."

The Shepherd and Clown approached.

The Shepherd said, "Come, boy. I'm past having more children, but your sons and daughters will be gentlemen born."

. . .

The Clown, now dressed finely, said, "See these clothes? Now say I'm no gentleman born. Try it!"

Autolycus acknowledged, "You are indeed a gentleman born."

The Clown boasted, "Yes, and have been for four hours."

The Shepherd agreed, "So have I, boy."

The Clown continued, "I was made a gentleman before my father. The king's son took my hand and called me brother. Then the two kings called my father brother. The prince and princess called my father father. We wept gentleman-like tears."

The Shepherd said, "We may live to shed more."

The Clown added, "Or else it's hard luck in our strange new status."

. . .

Autolycus humbly asked, "Please forgive my past faults and give me a good report to the prince."

The Shepherd urged, "Do, son. We must be gentle now."

The Clown asked, "Will you amend your life?"

Autolycus promised, "Yes, I will."

The Clown offered his hand, "I'll swear you're as honest as any in Bohemia."

The Shepherd cautioned, "You can say it, but not swear it."

The Clown insisted, "If it's false, a true gentleman can swear it for a friend. I'll swear you're a brave fellow and not a drunk, though I know otherwise."

Autolycus said, "I will prove to be a brave fellow."

. . .

The Clown said, "Then follow us. The kings and princes, our kin, are going to see the queen's statue. Come, we'll be your good masters."

They exited together.

SCENE 3

In a room in Paulina's house, Leontes, Polixenes, Florizel, Perdita, Camillo, Paulina, and their attendants gathered.

Leontes said, "Oh, dear Paulina, you have been such a comfort to me!"

Paulina responded, "What I did was not perfect, but I meant well. You have already thanked me, but having you, your brother the king, and your children visit my home is a great honor."

. . .

Leontes replied, "Oh, Paulina, we honor you with our visit. We came to see the statue of my queen. We saw many wonderful things, but we haven't yet seen the statue my daughter wants to see—the statue of her mother."

Paulina said, "Just like she was special in life, her statue is the best thing you will ever see. I kept it in a private place. Here it is. Get ready to see something amazing."

Paulina drew a curtain, revealing a statue of Hermione.

Leontes marveled, "It looks just like her! Oh, Hermione, if you can hear me, forgive me. This statue looks so real. But Paulina, Hermione wasn't this old."

Polixenes added, "Yes, she didn't look this old."

Paulina explained, "The artist made her look older, like she would if she were alive now."

. . .

Leontes reflected, "This statue reminds me of how she looked when I first fell in love with her. It's almost like she's alive. It's making me feel so many things."

Perdita asked, "Can I kneel and ask for her blessing? Dear queen, give me your hand to kiss."

Paulina cautioned, "Be patient! The paint is still fresh."

Camillo said, "My lord, your sorrow has lasted too long. No joy or sorrow should last so many years."

Polixenes added, "Dear brother, let me help take away some of your grief."

Paulina admitted, "If I had known this would make you so sad, I wouldn't have shown it."

Leontes said, "Do not draw the curtain."

. . .

Paulina responded, "I don't want you to get too upset."

Leontes insisted, "Let it be. Who made this statue? It looks like it's alive."

Polixenes praised, "The artist did an amazing job. It looks so real."

Leontes observed, "The eyes seem to move."

Paulina began to draw the curtain, "I'll cover it if it upsets you too much."

Leontes pleaded, "No, let me look at it longer."

Paulina said, "Either leave the chapel or prepare for more surprises. If you stay, I will make the statue move."

Leontes asked, "What do you mean? Make it move? I'm ready to see."

Paulina instructed, "You need to believe. Everyone stay still. Those who think it's wrong can leave."

Leontes declared, "Go ahead. No one will leave."

Paulina commanded, "Music, wake her up. It's time; move and come to life."

As music played, Hermione stepped down from her pedestal.

Paulina continued, "Don't be scared. She is alive. Give her your hand. You wooed her when she was young; now she comes to you."

Leontes exclaimed, "Oh, she's warm! If this is magic, it's wonderful."

Polixenes added, "She embraces him."

. . .

Camillo noted, "She hangs around his neck. If she is alive, let her speak."

Polixenes urged, "Yes, let her tell us where she has been."

Paulina explained, "It might seem unbelievable, but she is alive. Please kneel and ask for her blessing. Our Perdita is found."

Hermione blessed her daughter, "Dear gods, bless my daughter! Tell me, where have you been? How did you come to your father's court? I have kept myself alive to see this day."

Paulina intervened, "There's time for that later. Let's enjoy this happy moment. You all have won so much today. I will go to a quiet place and mourn my lost husband."

Leontes said, "Oh, peace, Paulina! You should remarry. I will help you find a good husband, just like you helped me find my queen."

. . .

He then said to everyone, "Let's leave this place. We need to talk about everything that has happened since we were separated. Lead us away, Paulina."

They all left together.

THE LIFE OF WILLIAM SHAKESPEARE

Step back in time with us as we discover the exciting life of **William Shakespeare**—a storyteller whose magnificent tales have been told and retold for hundreds of years. Fasten your seatbelts for some amazing facts about the Bard of Avon!

Birthday Mystery: Believe it or not, we don't know exactly when Shakespeare was born. Historians guess it was around April 23, 1564, but that's all because of the date of his baptism. How curious that such a famous person has a birthday shrouded in mystery!

. . .

School Days: Young Shakespeare attended the King's New School in his hometown, where he learned important subjects like Latin, Greek, history, and poetry—all without the gadgets and technology students have today.

Word Wizard: Shakespeare had a way with words, inventing over 1,700 of them! Imagine, every time you say "bedroom" or "excitement," you're using words that Shakespeare introduced to the English language.

Globe Trotter - But Not Really: The Globe Theatre is where Shakespeare's masterpieces were first performed—not a globe you can spin, but a large, round, open-air theater where audiences marveled under the sky.

Super-sized Works: Our dear Bard wrote 37 plays and 154 sonnets. That's a lot of storytelling! If you wrote a poem every week of the year, you'd still be short of Shakespeare's sonnet count.

Nicknamed "The Bard": Shakespeare is often referred to as "The Bard of Avon." 'Bard' means poet, and indeed, Shakespeare was a master poet from the town of Stratford-upon-Avon.

Lovey-Dovey Lines: Shakespeare's words about love are so beautiful that they are still read at weddings and shared between sweethearts today. And if you've heard the phrase "to be or not to be," you're quoting one of his most famous lines!

Queen for a Fan: Queen Elizabeth I loved the theater, and Shakespeare's plays were some of her most enjoyed performances. It was quite the honor for Shakespeare to entertain her majesty with his work.

Shakespeare's Secret Code: Some folks believe that Shakespeare tucked away secret codes within his plays—making each performance not just a show, but also a puzzle full of hidden meanings.

Goodnight, Sweet Prince: At age 52, in the year 1616, Shakespeare took his final bow. His presence may be missed, but his stories live on, continuing to inspire, entertain, and provoke thought across the globe.

. . .

So there you have it—a little peek into the life of the man who has kept us company through his words for over four centuries. Open the pages of his stories, and let William Shakespeare's plays transport you to a world where imagination knows no bounds. Happy reading!

It's hard for books to get noticed these days. Whether you liked this one or not, please consider writing a review, thanks!

Jeanette Vigon

SHAKESPEARE FOR KIDS - OTHER BOOKS IN THE SERIES

 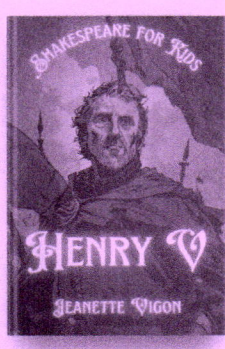 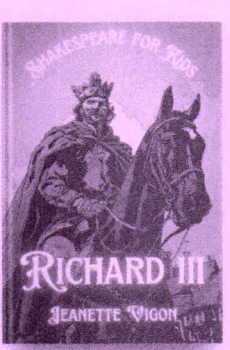

SHAKESPEARE FOR KIDS - OTHER BOOKS IN THE SERIES

SHAKESPEARE FOR KIDS - OTHER BOOKS IN THE SERIES

You can find the rest of the books in the series here:

https://amzn.to/3wLXpTC

Printed in Dunstable, United Kingdom